The Autobiography of Benjamin Franklin

A LOCHINVAR GUIDE

Student's Edition

EILEEN CUNNINGHAM

Edited by Amy Alexander Carmichael

LOCHINVAR GUIDES TO CLASSIC WORKS OF NONFICTION

Table of Contents

Introduction

We are thrilled that you have chosen *Lochinvar Guides* as your method of navigating the classic works of nonfiction in western civilization.

Methodology and Worldview

The *Guides* are informed by the classical method of education which emphasizes primary sources of history, the use of syllogistic thinking and logical analysis, and the application of the progymnasmata (early exercises in classical composition). Moreover, the *Guides* are written from a Christian worldview and incorporate Scripture throughout. There is, we believe, no basic incompatibility between these two paradigms. As the world entered the Christian Era, what made the classical method of education so highly adaptable to Christian culture was what Roman historian Cato the Elder (d. AD 149) posited as the purpose of education: to train up *"vir bonus, dicendi peritus"* (i.e., a good man speaking well)—the philosophy which Quinitillian used as his foundation in his educational treatise *Institutio Oratorio* (c. AD 95). From the time of Socrates, classical education has always driven students to ground themselves in morals and ethics; what could be more compatible with Christian education? Though in our own time Cato's nugget inspires the training not only of good men, but also good women, who, it is hoped, can both speak and *write* well. A program with such a methodology and such a purpose helps, we believe, to prepare students to follow in the footsteps of the great Christian orator, Paul of Tarsus, who wrote: "We destroy arguments and every lofty opinion raised against the knowledge of God, and take every thought captive to obey Christ" (2 Cor. 10:5).

Each work which is covered by one of the *Guides* is broken into manageable reading assignments, containing the following features:

- **Historical Background**—information that helps students better understand the work they are reading—e.g., the dynasty into which Charlemagne was born, the proprietary government of the British colonies in America, the Anglo-Saxon heptarchy in which King Alfred operated, etc.

- **Terms**—terms of a cultural or historical nature with which the general reader might not be familiar. What was a *chrisom*, for example? Or, what was the right of sanctuary?

- **Words**—vocabulary which might be new to the reader, presented with pronunciation key, part of speech, definition, and, if necessary, an explanation of archaic usage

- **Identifications**—identifications of people, places, and events which may be unfamiliar. Who were the Merovingians, for example? Or, where is St. George's Channel?

- **Illustrations**—portraits or classic works of art that can foster a more personal response than unillustrated material can

- **Questions**—short answer questions, plus "graduated questions," wherein the student answers a series of objective questions (grammar stage, in the classical tradition) which lead to more subjective questions (logic or rhetoric stage)

- **Diction Analysis**—highlights of effective stylistic techniques which elevate the work above others of its type

- **Nonfiction Strategies**—activities designed to improve certain skills useful in the reading of nonfiction: following transitions, analyzing verb tense, perceiving tone, generating images, taking notes, etc.

- **Adapted Literature Circle Approaches**—special activities which lead the student to make connections, think critically, etc. (see full details below)

- **Composition Topics**—writing about ideas generated by the text; sometimes employing elements of the progymnasmata (the early exercises in classical composition) for which approaches and models are explained

Depending on the class or the individual home school student, a teacher or teaching parent can pick and choose from among the various options—or even substitute alternative topics for research or composition. *Lochinvar Guides* are intended to stimulate readers to want to learn more, so we are happy if you are stimulated to research something of personal meaning to you.

Literature Circle Approaches in the *Lochinvar Guides*

Classroom teachers often use Literature Circles in order to provide their students with a full reading experience. In such a case, a class is divided into small groups, or "circles," and as the days roll by, students take turns serving as Illustrator, Connector, Word Master, Quiz Master, or Researcher. In the *Lochinvar Guides,* the technique has been adapted somewhat to make it useful in either a classroom or a home-school setting. It is our fondest hope that students will develop a lifelong desire to go beyond the text at hand and broaden out to other resources, including, in the case of Illustrator, their own imaginations. Below is a brief explanation of each approach.

Illustration—One of the differences between watching a movie and reading a book is that viewers passively absorb an image imposed by another person while readers actively create pictures in their own minds. This is one of the great pleasures of reading—seeing with "the mind's eye." In works of nonfiction, the imaging goes beyond entertainment, which is perhaps the focus of literature, and helps the reader better understand people, places, and events from real life—battlefields and battle formations, for example, or Greek architecture or Roman roads. To this end, students are asked from time to time to examine a particular passage for its visual detail and render it on a piece of paper (stick figures are altogether fine). Examples might be to sketch a person who has gotten himself into a predicament, a genealogical chart, a map, a graph, etc.

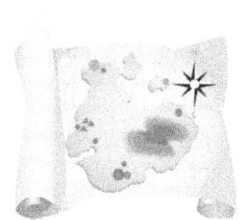

Research—Sometimes an author will introduce a topic but not provide all the details. In these cases, you will be directed to find out more about a topic in a library or on the Internet. For example, Benjamin Franklin lived in Pennsylvania, where there was a large Quaker population often mentioned by Franklin in his autobiography. A suitable research topic would be to discover some of the basic facts about the Quaker religion.

Connection—"Great minds think alike," runs an old saying. They may not always think exactly alike, but they do often think about the same things. If, for example, while reading a first-person account of a war experience, one might come across the explanation of a deception

that was played on the enemy. This might put the reader in mind of the Trojan horse narrative from the *Iliad* or the *Aeneid*. This link-up would connect the text with a work of literature, but connections can also be made with current events, historic events, aphorisms, music, movies—or even personal experience.

Bible Connection—One special kind of connection is, of course, connection with Scripture. In 2 Corinthians 10:5, Paul states, "We destroy arguments and every lofty opinion raised against the knowledge of God, and take every thought captive to obey Christ." Therefore, as part of their intellectual life, Christian readers frequently ask, "Does the message comport with or contradict Scripture?" Even when reading works of the ancient philosophers who did not have the advantage of revealed religion, we sometimes come across statements that are markedly prescient regarding the biblical narrative. The narrative referred to as "Plato's Cave," for example, is astonishingly insightful. As Cyril of Jerusalem put it so long ago, the Father, the Son, and the Holy Spirit "lighteneth *every* man coming into the world"[1] (emphasis mine). Discovering glimpses of ultimate truth (or the lack thereof) among both ancient and modern writers makes familiarity with and application of Scripture an invaluable tool for the believer.

Mortimer Adler's 102 Great Ideas—Mortimer Adler's contribution to the study of the Great Books was monumental. You will find a more detailed explanation of the use of his 102 Great Ideas in the pages that follow. Here it is only necessary to know that, like works of literature, great works of nonfiction also deal with universal themes—ideas that are relevant at all times to all people. From time to time, you will be asked to examine a passage by a particular writer in light of one of the topics form Adler's list, such as War, Progress, Courage, Law, or Justice. In this way, you will be able to engage in what Adler called the Great Conversation of western civilization.

The 102 Great Ideas Identified by Mortimer Adler

1. Angel	27. Fate	53. Matter	79. Religion
2. Animal	28. Form	54. Mechanics	80. Revolution
3. Aristocracy	29. God	55. Medicine	81. Rhetoric
4. Art	30. Good and Evil	56. Memory and Imagination	82. Same and Other
5. Astronomy and Cosmology	31. Government	57. Metaphysics	83. Science
6. Beauty	32. Habit	58. Mind	84. Sense
7. Being	33. Happiness	59. Monarchy	85. Sign and Symbol
8. Cause	34. History	60. Nature	86. Sin
9. Chance	35. Habit	61. Necessity and Contingency	87. Slavery
10. Change	36. Hypothesis	62. Oligarchy	88. Soul
11. Citizen	37. Idea	63. One and Many	89. Space
12. Constitution	38. Immortality	64. Opinion	90. State
13. Courage	39. Induction	65. Opposition	91. Temperance
14. Custom and Convention	40. Infinity	66. Philosophy	92. Theology
15. Definition	41. Judgment	67. Physics	93. Time
16. Democracy	42. Justice	68. Pleasure and Pain	94. Truth
17. Desire	43. Knowledge	69. Poetry	95. Tyranny and Despotism
18. Dialectic	44. Labor	70. Principle	96. Universal and Particular
19. Duty	45. Language	71. Progress	97. Virtue and Vice
20. Education	46. Law	72. Prophecy	98. War and Peace
21. Element	47. Liberty	73. Prudence	99. Wealth
22. Emotion	48. Life and Death	74. Punishment	100. Will
23. Eternity	49. Logic	75. Quality	101. Wisdom
24. Evolution	50. Love	76. Quantity	102. World
25. Experience	51. Man (Humankind)	77. Reasoning	
26. Family	52. Mathematics	78. Relation	

The Use of Adler's 102 Great Ideas in *Lochinvar Guides to Classic Works of Nonfiction*

Mortimer Adler

As part of his effort to improve education by improving the way students think, the American philosopher and educator Mortimer Adler (1902-2001), founded, with Max Weissman, the Center for the Study of the Great Ideas. In doing so, scholars identified what Adler called the 102 Great Ideas, which he defined as "the ideas basic and indispensable to understanding ourselves, our society, and the world in which we live."[2]

In their English classes at school, students are usually introduced to the concept of *theme,* that is, the idea which a given work of literature develops. In this respect, Adler's list can be quite helpful. In *Romeo and Juliet* by William Shakespeare, for example, students might discuss exactly what it was that made things go so wrong for the young, "star-crossed" lovers. Were they really destined by their stars, or were they ruined by the bad choices of the humans in the story? These questions correspond to at least two of the Great Ideas on Adler's list: Fate and Cause. Therefore, the list of the 102 Great Ideas can certainly help you respond to the theme underlying a great work of literature.

But what about great works of nonfiction, especially the primary sources of history—autobiographies, eyewitness accounts of history, philosophical treatises, laws and charters, *enchiridia,* and the like? Can Adler's list of the Great Ideas help the student with these works? We believe so. It is the purpose of the *Lochinvar Guides to Classic Works of Nonfiction* to help students to think about the ideas underlying the important nonfiction works of the western canon. Specifically, we hope you will learn, first, to read not only for facts, but for ideas; and, secondly, not only for comprehension of the ideas, but for a rigorous examination of them.

Why "rigorous examination"? *Lochinvar Guides* are written from a classical and Christian point of view. We wholeheartedly agree with the apostle Paul, who pointed out that we no longer have to be "tossed back and forth by the waves, and blown here and there by every wind of teaching" nor need we fall victim to "the cunning and craftiness of people in their deceitful scheming" (Eph. 4:14).

What is more, we are even commanded to evaluate ideas: "Do not despise prophecies, but test everything; hold fast what is good" (I Thess. 5:20-21). And the

God of Abraham, Isaac, and Jacob has shown that he does not shy away from any test. In the Old Testament, for example, we see that God allowed Jacob to wrestle with him; and in the New Testament, we see that the risen Jesus allowed the doubting disciple Thomas examine his wounds. In neither case was the mere mortal—so full of questions—judged or condemned. Rather, God was not offended because he knew that he would triumph in any contest regarding Truth.

In short, we are not only encouraged, but even commanded to question the voices in the wind, and, because Judeo-Christian Scripture is solid ground, we know we can use it as our bedrock in the storm. That is why you will be asked in these study guides not only to search for a writer's ideas and to test them by using reason and logic, but also to evaluate them in the light of Scripture.

One last question remains: When we refer to the *Great Ideas*, what exactly is meant by the word *great*? For example, noticing that Slavery is on the list, one might say that slavery was not at all a great idea, that it was—and remains—a horrible idea. To sort this all out, we can turn to the work of Peter Mark Roget (1779-1869), the creator of *Roget's International Thesaurus*, who suggested the following synonyms for the word *great*: *important, consequential, prominent; noteworthy, memorable; weighty, solemn, serious;* and, for the word *weighty*, he suggests *influential*.[3] All of these synonyms help explain Adler's application of the word *great*. He did not necessarily mean each Idea was *wonderful*, but that it was *consequential, weighty,* or *influential*—for better or for worse. It is in this sense, then, that we can see that Evil, Slavery, and Tyranny properly belong among Adler's 102 Great Ideas alongside Truth, Beauty, and Love.

Recommended Text

There are many editions of the *Autobiography of Benjamin Franklin* available, both online and in print. We have divided the readings into sections that can be used with any version of the text, but for easiest reference, we recommend the Penguin Classics edition (ISBN 978-0142437605).

Historical Background

The English have their Alfred the Great; the Russians, their Peter the Great; and the French, of course, their Charlemagne (Latin for Charles the Great). What's more, the habit of dubbing monarchs "the Great" is not confined to Europe. The Bible narrates the deeds of a man called Herod the Great, and the Arabs regale the deeds of Suleiman the Magnificent (again, *magnificent* being based on the Latin *magna*, or *great*). What's more, England's Elizabeth the Great and Russia's Catherine the Great testify that the practice is not confined to men only.

As Americans with a more democratic spirit, though we may honor our leaders, we tend not to glorify them with such monikers. After hearing of the death of Benjamin Franklin, the French Comte de Mirabeau, who had been a moderate voice in the French Revolution, certainly expressed the attitude of a Republic toward such a great man, saying of Franklin, "Antiquity would have raised altars to this mighty genius who, to the advantage of mankind, compassing in his mind the heavens and the earth, was able to restrain alike thunderbolts and tyrants."[4]

So how can Americans make a visible show of their undying admiration for a person who has been important in their national story? One way, of course, has been to erect a statue. Another has been to place the person's image on the nation's currency. Benjamin Franklin, of course, has been honored in both ways with at least ten statues and his image on the $100 bill, so it behooves us who live in the country he helped to create to discover what was so special about this man, whom another generation would have dubbed "Benjamin the Great."

To understand the world of Ben Franklin (1706-1790) and the problems facing his generation, it is important to remember that, although he lived to be eighty-four years old, the first seventy years of his life were lived not in a place called the United States, but in colonies belonging to the Crown of England—mainly Massachusetts and Pennsylvania. He was by no means among the first Englishman on the continent. Jamestown had been founded in 1607 (100 years before his birth) and the Plymouth Bay Colony in 1620, but towns on the European model were still being carved out of the wilderness in young Ben's time.

We might best understand the challenges of his time if we imagine what the first settlers on the moon or planet Mars would have to do to establish American colonies in space. That, of course, would be an even more daunting task since there would almost certainly be no natural resources—or even air to breathe! But the task of building towns and establishing all the institutions that it takes to run them (from schools to hospitals to police) would certainly put us in mind of the daunting task facing the first colonists on the American continent.

Benjamin Franklin, citizen of Philadelphia, played no small role in that effort. Without him, it is hard to say how things would have developed or how much longer it might have taken to establish well-managed cities. Franklin's accomplishment in the establishment of Philadelphia was acknowledged in 1938 by his biographer Carl Van Doren, who said, "No other town burying its great man, ever buried more of itself than Philadelphia with Franklin,"[5] and, in a way, the same can be said of the nation as a whole.

Just one topic more remains to provide the historical background you might need to understand Franklin's milieu. As mentioned above, Franklin was for the first seventy years of his life a British subject, and the long-established British principle of landholding held sway on this continent until the Revolution. That is to say, all land belonged to the king, and he divided it up as he pleased, awarding dukedoms and earldoms to whomever he chose—and only as long as they continued to support him in return. On the American side of the Atlantic, the king established four kinds of colonies, one of which was a *proprietary colony,* the care of which the king would place in the hands of a loyalist who would see to its business and handle its investments.

In Pennsylvania, the proprietor was William Penn (1644-1718). Penn's father, Admiral Sir William Penn, had been instrumental in returning to the English throne the exiled heir, King Charles II, whose father, Charles I, had been executed by the Puritan Parliament and leader, Oliver Cromwell. As a way of thanking the Admiral, Charles awarded his (Penn's) son the proprietorship of an American colony, which the young man wished to call Sylvania (Latin for *woods*) due to the many forests of spruce, fir, birch, pine and alder. (Even today, the state preserves 2.2 million acres of forest, and, of course, the legendary Big Foot is said to reside thereabouts.)

King Charles decided to add Penn's name to the word *sylvania* (woods), naming the colony Pennsylvania (or Penn's Woods), which, though it is said to have caused Penn some embarrassment, became the official name of the colony.

Now, the way this all relates to Benjamin Franklin is this: William Penn had become a Quaker at the age of 22, after developing sympathies for the persecuted sect at Oxford. Quakers are pacifists, and one of the first things William Penn did in Pennsylvania, after his arrival in October 1682, was to meet with Native Americans of the Lenape tribe and establish a bond of friendship with them, an event commemorated in a famous painting by

Penn's Treaty with the Indians by Benjamin West

Benjamin West called *Penn's Treaty with the Indians* (shown above right). As the French philosopher Voltaire put it in 1733, the agreement between Penn and the Lenape was "the only treaty between those people and the Christians that was not ratified by an oath, and was never infring'd."[6]

Of course, Penn eventually passed away, and not all Indians in the region were Lenape. In Franklin's time, when the Pennsylvania colonists were suffering from raids and massacres at the hands of the Delawares in the 1750s and '60s, the settlers appealed to the colonial government at Philadelphia for assistance. Here is where the pacifist Quakers came into conflict with Franklin and others who advocated a tax to support a defensive campaign. As you read, you will see how both Franklin and the Quakers handled themselves in this impasse.

In summary, Franklin's world comprised the proprietary government of the Crown, the Quakers, the settlers, and the Native Americans. Franklin's narrative will take you there as a virtual eyewitness to the events of the time.

Part 1: Family and Youth

Scope

This reading covers pp. 3-24a in the Penguin edition.

Terms

In this and subsequent chapters, the terms, words, and identifications are presented in alphabetical order.

1. apprentice (n.) – a person who is learning a trade

2. Assembly (n.) – the governing body of the colony of Pennsylvania, begun by William Penn in 1682 and consisting of four members from each county elected by freemen

3. indenture (n.) – a contract in which a young person in training is bound to a master of the craft or trade (such as printing)

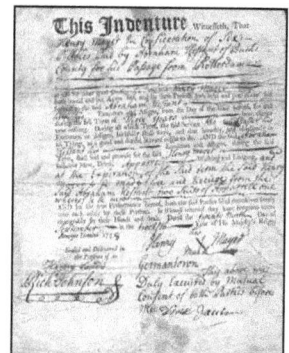

An Indenture of 1738

4. journeyman (n.) – a person who has finished apprenticeship training in a trade or craft, but has not yet reached the rank of master

5. Nonconformity (n.) – religious views that differed from those of the Church of England, which was the official religion of the realm

6. "old style" and "new style" calendars (n.) – the Julian (old) and Gregorian (new) calendars. Britain and her colonies accepted the new calendar in 1752.

7. Socratic method (n.) – a method of argumentation, named after the Greek philosopher Socrates, in which one asks questions in order to draw out truths and insights into the issue at hand

Words

8. conventicle [kən-VĔN-tĭ-kəl] (n.) – a secret or unlawful meeting, especially of a religious group

9. dogmatical [dŏg-MĂT-ĭ-kəl] (adj.) – (more often written as *dogmatic*) of or relating to religious dogma, a set body of principles taught by a religious group; sometimes used as a pejorative, suggesting inflexibility

Identifications

10. Mather – the Reverend Doctor Cotton Mather (1663-1678), an influential Puritan minister and author associated with the Massachusetts Bay Colony

11. *The Spectator* - a daily publication founded by Joseph Addison and Richard Steele in England in the early 18th century with the goal of bringing "philosophy out of closets and libraries, schools, and colleges, to dwell in clubs and assemblies, at tea-tables and coffee–houses"[7]

The Rev. Dr. Cotton Mather

Questions

1. Use the diagram of graduated questions on the next page to assess Franklin's explanation of the political and religious environment in England in the time of his ancestors.

a. **Grammar Question:** At the time of the Reformation and through the reign of Queen Mary, the Franklins: (a) became Protestant; (b) remained Roman Catholic. (PENGUIN 6)

b. **Grammar Question:** In the time of Charles II, Ben's father, Josiah, and uncle, Benjamin: (a) joined Non-Conformist conventicles; (b) stayed with the Church of England (Episcopal Church). (PENGUIN 7)

c. **Grammar Question:** After the conventicles became illegal, Josiah Franklin: (a) continued with the Church of England; (b) emigrated for freedom of religion. (PENGUIN 7)

d. **Grammar Question:** Benjamin's maternal grandfather, Peter Folger: (a) supported the Church of England (Episcopals); (b) opposed discrimination against Baptists, Quakers, etc. (PENGUIN 7)

e. **Logic Question:** What conclusions can you draw about the religious and political environment of the age?

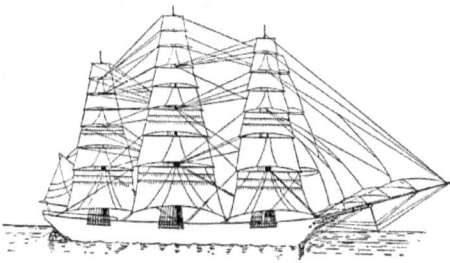

2. Which phrase best describes the Franklin family when they were still in England? (PENGUIN 4-6)

   a. peasant farm workers

   b. landed gentry

   c. tradesmen and craftsmen

   d. nobility

3. What pastimes did Franklin greatly enjoy as a lad and with his friend Collins? (PENGUIN 12, 13)

4. Franklin enjoyed reading and debating with his friends, but he shares a bit of advice about such arguments. In the space below, use your own words to explain the warning he gives to "well-meaning sensible men" (PENGUIN 16-17)?

5. How did it come to pass that Ben, the younger brother, got management of his brother's paper, *The New England Courant?* (PENGUIN 18-20)

6. In one or two sentences, explain how it came to pass that young Ben left Boston without telling anyone of his plan. (PENGUIN 20-21)

7. After nonchalantly narrating how he saved a drowning Dutchman, Franklin moves on to a discussion of a book which was in the man's pocket. He states it was an "old favorite," and indeed it is considered a Christian classic. (PENGUIN 22)

    a. The title was _____; the author was _____

    b. According to Franklin, it was the first book to _____

    _____

Nonfiction Reading Skill: Following Sequence

Though autobiography is a form of nonfiction, it differs from other forms of nonfiction in that it is told in narrative style in much the same way as a fictional story is told. Main ideas are not always stated in topic sentences at the beginning of a paragraph. Instead, the writer will narrate life events using chronological order, that is, the order of time. Several techniques are available to the writer of narrative fiction, and readers with an understanding of the techniques can more easily navigate the waters.

As an example, we can analyze statements from the New Testament narratives regarding the arrest, trial, and crucifixion of Jesus, noting the chronological techniques employed by the Gospel writers:

1. **Direct transitions** which support chronological order are adverbs of time.

    - **Simple transitions** (e.g., *at first, then, later, prior to that,* and *after that*)

    - **Adverb clauses** (e.g., *before Jesus was taken to Pilate; after the cock crowed three times*).

    Mark 15:33-34 *"And **when the sixth hour had come**, there was darkness over the whole land **until the ninth hour**. And **at the ninth hour** Jesus cried with a loud voice, 'Eloi, Eloi, lema sabachthani?'"*

2. **Verb tense** which supports chronology.

    - **Simple Past for sequential action:**

    Mark 15:16-17 *"And the soldiers **led** him away inside the palace (that is, the governor's headquarters), and they **called** together the whole battalion. And they **clothed** him in a purple cloak. . . ."*

    - **Past Progressive + Simple Past for interrupted action:**

    Luke 22:60b-61a *"And immediately, while he **was** still **speaking**, the rooster **crowed**. And the Lord **turned** and **looked** at Peter. And Peter **remembered** the saying of the Lord."*

- **Past Progressive for continuous action:**

  Mark 15:18-19 *"And they began to salute him, 'Hail, King of the Jews!' And they **were striking** his head with a reed and **spitting** on him and **kneeling** down in homage to him."*

- **Past Progressive for simultaneous action:**

  Luke 22:63 *"Now the men who **were holding** Jesus in custody **were mocking** him as they beat him."*

- **Past Perfect + Simple Past for prior action:**

  Mark 15:20a *"And when they **had mocked** him, they **stripped** him of the purple cloak and **put** his own clothes on him."*

By following clues such as adverbs and verb tense, readers can improve their comprehension of material involving (a) narrative sequencing; (b) cause-effect; and (c) steps in a process, to name a few. In the exercise below, you will be able to apply your understanding of chronological order by examining a passage by Benjamin Franklin in which he explains how he solved a problem, the first of many such passages in the autobiography. Though he never announces his purpose with a topic sentence such as, "Let me show you how I solved a problem," the savvy reader will intuitively grasp the purpose of his chronological narrative.

Exercise 1: Following Sequence

Directions: Please begin by reading the introductory material and reviewing the passage in the autobiography. Then fulfill the task in the space provided below.

Introduction to the Task

Benjamin Franklin once said, "Without continual growth and progress, such words as *improvement, achievement,* and *success* have no meaning." In adulthood, Franklin proved himself a brilliant problem-solver, but even in this early section of the autobiography, we see that as a young man, he was able to devise strategies for self-improvement.

Take, for example, the passage that begins with Franklin's narrative of his debates with his friend Collins.

- The author observes, "*He (Collins) was naturally more eloquent. . . .*" (PENGUIN 14)

- He continues for two more paragraphs and concludes with the phrase "*of which I was extremely ambitious*" (PENGUIN 15).

Read through this passage with a focus on Franklin's problem-solving process. Use chronological transitions and verb tense to keep track of the first step, the second step, and so on. In the space provided, make a list of the steps Franklin used to solve his problem. You may find that some of the steps have sub-steps. Then compare your list of steps to that of another student to see if you read it in the same way. Your teacher may want to make a master list of the steps on the board to facilitate the conversation.

Task Response

The Great Ideas: Religion and Reasoning

Two of the 102 Great Ideas laid out by Mortimer Adler are **Religion** and **Reasoning**. As Franklin narrated his life, he often commented about his spiritual journey, yet he was a man of his times, and during the Enlightenment in the seventeenth and eighteenth century, more emphasis was put on human reason than on revealed religion. We will follow Franklin's thoughts on these matters as we proceed through his book, but we can begin with a look at what happened when Franklin began to use Socratic dialogue to question others about their religious beliefs. What effect did this have on Franklin's own religious thinking and his life relationships with others? (PENGUIN 16-17, 21).

Research

In a library book or on the Internet, research the value of the various British coins in use in the eighteenth century. One good web site is *Learn NC,* sponsored by the University of North Carolina at Chapel Hill, in which you will find Section 6.5 "The Value of Money in Colonial America" by David Walbert. URL: <http://www.learnnc.org/lp/editions/nchist-colonial/1646>.

Part 2: To Philadelphia

Scope

This reading covers pp. 24b-42a in the Penguin edition.

Terms

1. "letter of credit" (n. phr.) – a letter from a bank (or, in Franklin's narrative, an individual person) which promises to pay a seller in full within a given time period

2. piece of eight (n. phr.) – a silver coin minted in Spain having a value of eight *reals* [rā-ÄLZ] (the main Spanish currency); the first global currency

Spanish real of 1768

3. proprietary [pro-PRĪ-ə-tār-ē] (n.) – a person who held land by a right given by the king of England in his American colonies, in much the same way as a duke held land in England

Words

4. approbation [ăp-rō-BĀ-shən] (n.) - approval

5. parsimony [PÄR-sĭ-mō-nē] (n.) – stinginess, unwillingness to spend or lend money

6. stationer [STĀ-shən-ər] (n.) – a person who sells writing materials such as paper and pens

Identifications

7. Barbados [bar-BĀ-dōs] (n.) – an island under British control in the Caribbean, spelled by Franklin as *Barbadoes*.

8. Pope – the surname of the English poet, Alexander Pope (1688-1744)

9. Quaker [KWĀK-ər] (n.) – a member of the Quaker religion, the Religious Society of Friends, founded in the mid-seventeenth century by George Fox (1624-91) in England. Quakers were heavily persecuted there. Since Penn, a Quaker, founded Pennsylvania (Penn's woods), numerous Quakers emigrated there.

Questions

1. Franklin describes his sad condition and appearance upon his arrival in Philadelphia. In the space below, draw a sketch which shows the way Franklin describes himself as he leaves the bakery where he has spent three pennies (PENGUIN 25). (Stick figures are okay.)

2. In a few words, describe Franklin's impressions of the printers and printing houses in Philadelphia (PENGUIN 26-27).

3. On the next page, answer the series of graduated questions, carrying the facts forward to the logic question at the end.

Graduated Questions

a. **Grammar Question:** Sir William Keith, governor of the province, is impressed with young Ben and proposes that Ben should start what? (PENGUIN 28-29)

b. **Grammar Question:** The reaction of Franklin's father to this proposal is to refuse—on what grounds? (PENGUIN 30)

c. **Grammar Question:** When Sir William hears of the reaction of Mr. Franklin, what does he offer? (PENGUIN 34)

d. **Grammar Question:** Upon his arrival in England, what does Franklin find out? (PENGUIN 40)

e. **Grammar Question:** In the meantime, how was Franklin's friendship with Collins challenged? (PENGUIN 32-33)

f. **Logic Question:** Drawing on your answers to questions *d* and *e*, explain how Franklin's father was proven correct (question *b*)?

Sir William Keith
Colonial Governor of Pennsylvania

Research

Time and place interact to create human history. In this case, we find ourselves in Philadelphia, Pennsylvania, in the eighteenth century. In this respect, we should not be surprised to find frequent references to the Quakers. On the Internet or in the library, do some research to learn seven basic facts about this faith.

**William Penn
(1644-1718)**

1. Founder:

2. Place and date of origin:

3. Attitude toward war:

4. Characteristic of church services:

5. Treatment in England:

6. Areas where Quakers settled in America:

7. Meaning of the name of the city "Philadelphia":

Part 3: To London

Scope

This reading covers pp. 42b-70a in the Penguin edition.

Terms

1. Dissenting [dĭs-SĔNT-ĭng] (adj.) – standing in opposition to the Church of England; a person who did this was termed a Dissenter.

2. pistole [pĭs-TŌL] (n.) – any golden coin minted in a European country and in circulation in the 17th and 18th centuries; worth slightly less than a British pound

3. Romish [RŌM-ĭsh] (adj.) – of or relating to the Roman Catholic Church; slightly derogatory

Words

4. distemper [dĭs-TĔM-pər] (n.) – illness (18th century usage, now archaic)

5. pleurisy [PLŪ-rĭ-sē] (n.) – a medical condition caused by inflammation in the lungs

6. metaphysical [mĕt-ə-FĬZ-ĭ-kəl] (adj.) – of or relating to metaphysics, which is a branch of philosophy that explores the essence of being and knowing

Identifications

7. Lincoln's Inn Fields (n. phr.) – the largest public square in London

8. Deist [DĒ-ĭst] (n.) – a person who practices Deism, a religious philosophy that views God as the Creator but not an active participant in history

Questions

1. How did Franklin earn money while in London? (PENGUIN 42)

2. What athletic skill of Franklin's do we learn about in this section? (PENGUIN 48)

3. Franklin is remembered as an inventor. In this section, he mentions some of the things he invented. Please list them below:

   a. (PENGUIN 43) _____

   b. (PENGUIN 53)_____ and _____

   c. (PENGUIN 55) _____

4. Housed in the same London house as Franklin, a Roman Catholic woman lived a quiet life devoted to prayer and contemplation, yet she still offered her confession to a priest every day. Franklin wondered why a woman with so little opportunity to sin would need to confess daily.

   a. **Fact:** What was her answer? (PENGUIN 47)
      "

   b. **Bible Connection:** Does Scripture support her answer? Provide the verse reference that underlies your response.

Bible Connection

Franklin continues to draw attention to behaviors that get his friends into trouble. Answer the series of graduated questions about his friends, carrying the thoughts forward to the Bible connection at the end. (John Collins' behaviors from the previous reading have been provided for you as an example in Fact 1.)

Fact 1: What two behaviors on the part of his friend caused Ben and John Collins finally to fall out? (PENGUIN 32)

Drinking and gambling

Fact 2: What behaviors seemed to stain the character of James Ralph? (PENGUIN 39, 43-44).

Fact 3: What fault in himself does Franklin blame on his "being . . . under no religious restraints" at that time in his life? (PENGUIN 44)

Fact 4: What problem did Franklin see among the other employees at Watt's Printing House? (PENGUIN 45)

Fact 5: What weaknesses did George Webb exhibit that caused his hopes of success in London to fail? (PENGUIN 53)

Fact 6: Why did Franklin dub his acquaintance Samuel Mickle a "croaker"? (PENGUIN 53)

Bible Connection: Choose two of the vices that Franklin mentioned above and find passages of Scripture which provide moral instruction.

Discuss with your class: (a) Why did Franklin spurn these behaviors? (b) Why might a believer in God deem them a problem?

The Great Ideas: Industry

One of the 102 Great Ideas laid out by Mortimer Adler is **Industry.** This term does not refer to industry in the sense of manufacturing (e.g., the clothing industry). Rather, it refers to the manner in which human beings apply themselves to their work. Franklin addresses this theme directly in a passage that begins immediately after the discussion of his group, the Junto. Please re-read from "But my giving this Account of it here. . . ." to "see its Effects in my favor throughout this Relation" (PENGUIN 60-61). Then state, in your own words, what you perceive to be Franklin's thoughts on the theme of Industry.

Research

In this section, we read about George Webb, a former Oxford University student, who came to America by indenture. In this narrative, Franklin makes reference to "Crimp's Bill" (PENGUIN 53). On the Internet or in a library, do research to discover what these are: (a) an indenture; (b) crimp's bill, or "crimping."

Part 4: Virtue

Scope

This reading covers pp. 70b-93a in the Penguin edition.

Words

1. porringer [PÔR-ĭn-jər] (n.) – a small bowl, often with a small handle, used for eating soup, stew, etc.

Identifications

2. Addison [ĂD-ĭ-sən] (n.) – Joseph Addison (1672-1719), an English essayist and poet, who wrote a tragedy about Marcus Porcius Cato Uticensis (95-46 BC), a Roman statesman

3. Cicero [SĬS-ə-rō] (n.) – Marcus Tullius Cicero (106-43 BC), a Roman statesman, orator, and writer

4. Pythagoras [pĭ-THĂG-ər-əs] – a Greek philosopher and mathematician who lived c.582-c.500 BC

5. Tacitus [TĂS-ĭ-təs] (n.) – a Roman historian who lived AD c.55-c.120

Questions

1. What was the purpose of the letter from Mr. Benjamin Vaughn? (PENGUIN 70-71)

_____

2. What did Franklin establish at Philadelphia, and how did he find funds to do so? (PENGUIN 77-78)

3. How did Franklin compensate for his lack of formal education? (PENGUIN 79)

4. Franklin quotes a Bible verse that he said proved true in his life (PENGUIN 79). However, it is quoted from the King James Bible, and since Franklin's time, the language has changed enough that the meaning is somewhat unclear. Begin by copying the verse in the space provided. Then consult a Bible such as the English Standard Version (ESV), the New International Version (NIV), or the New King James Version (NKJV) and copy in the space the more readable translation.

Proverbs 22:29 (as it appears in the text): _____

_____

Newer translation: _____ _____

_____

_____

_____

The Great Ideas: Religion

In this reading, Franklin continues discussing the development of his religious views. Examine his expansion by answering the following questions:

1. What did Franklin consider to be "the Essentials of every Religion"? (PENGUIN 80) (Feel free to condense his wording into a short phrase or a single word.)

a. _____

b. _____

c. _____

d. _____

e. _____

f. _____

2. What was Franklin's attitude toward other religions? (PENGUIN 80)

3. What does he say about attendance at church? (PENGUIN 81)

The Great Ideas: Virtue

1. One of the 102 Great Ideas laid out by Mortimer Adler is **Virtue**. In this reading, Franklin describes his "Project of arriving at moral Perfection." Briefly explain his project (PENGUIN 82-88) and summarize his results (PENGUIN 89-90). (*NOTE:* It is not necessary to copy all the virtues he lists; just provide a few examples.)

2. When a Quaker told him he was too proud, what virtue did Franklin add to his list, and how did it affect the way he conversed with his friends?

Part 5: Building Philadelphia

This reading covers pp. 93b-112a in the Penguin edition.

TERMS

1. mufti [MŬF-tē] (n.) – a Muslim scholar who interprets the law of the Koran

WORDS

2. gaol (jāl) – British spelling of *jail*

IDENTIFICATIONS

3. Constantinople [kän-stăn-tn-Ō-pəl] – former capital of the Eastern Roman Empire, Constantinople (today known as Istanbul) came under Ottoman Muslim control in 1431

4. Mahometanism [mə-HŎM-ə-tn-ĭzm] (n.) – Islam, the religion established by Mohammad

5. Moravian [mä-RĀ-vē-ən] (n.) – the oldest Protestant denomination, formed in the fifteenth century in the area now known as the Czech Republic

6. Whitefield [WHĬT-fēld] (n.) – Rev. George Whitefield (see image), a Church of England preacher (1714-70) prominent in the Great Awakening movement in the colonial period; one of the founders of the Methodist Church

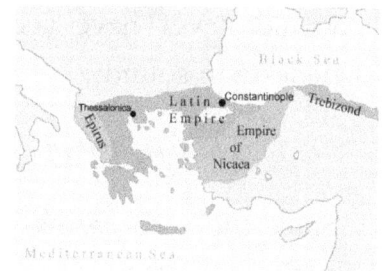

The Rev. George Whitefield

Diction: Absolute Constructions

One method of expressing sequence in a narrative is the absolute construction. An absolute construction can be defined as a noun or pronoun working with a participial phrase in a dependent structure that has no grammatical connection to the main clause. Here is an example from the writing of Benjamin Franklin:

The sloop putting in at New Port, Rhode Island, I visited my brother John, who had been married and settled there some years.

The absolute construction consists of the following parts:

- Noun (*the sloop*)

- Participle (*putting in*)

- Prepositional Phrase (*at New Port, Rhode Island*)

Actually, the absolute construction is the reduction of a complete sentence:

The sloop put in at New Port, Rhode Island.

However, if Franklin had just strung simple sentences together with *and then*, his work would never have achieved the status of a classic. It would have a much more pedestrian sound:

The sloop put in at New Port, Rhode Island, and then I visited my brother. . . .

Since the verb *put* has been reduced to the participle *putting*, one might wonder why such a construction is not simply called a participial phrase. The answer is that the absolute construction contains its own subject—in this case, the noun *sloop*.

Since cause-effect relationships also depend on sequencing (first the cause, then the effect), nonfiction writers sometimes employ the absolute construction when explaining why a certain action was taken. Here is another example from Ben Franklin:

So we put towards the shore, got into a creek, landed near an old fence with the rails of which we made a fire, *the night being cold.* . . .

The absolute construction (*the night being cold*) shows the reason why the travelers made a fire: *because the night was cold.* Since Franklin favors the absolute construction in his writing, it is not surprising to see him express the reason in this way.

Exercise: Decoding Absolute Constructions

<u>Directions</u>: Four of Benjamin Franklin's sentences from this section appear below with the absolute construction appearing in italic print. In the space provided, turn the absolute construction into an adverb clause using *since* or *because* to express the reason for the action.

Example:

> So we put towards the shore, got into a creek, landed near an old fence with the rails of which we made a fire, *the night being cold. . . .*
>
> *. . . because the night was cold.*

1. I therefore filled all the little spaces that occurred between the remarkable days in the calendar, with proverbial sentences, chiefly such as inculcated industry and frugality, as the means of procuring wealth and thereby securing virtue, *it being more difficult for a man in want to act always honestly. . .* (PENGUIN 96).

2. *The contributions being made by people of different sects promiscuously,* care was taken in the nomination of trustees to avoid giving a predominancy to any sect, so that one of each was appointed. . . (PENGUIN 106).

3. *The partnership at Carolina having succeeded,* I was encouraged to engage in others, and to promote several of my workmen who had behaved well, by establishing them with printing houses in different colonies, on the same terms with that in Carolina (PENGUIN 109).

More challenging: The next example contains *two* absolute constructions to express two reasons for Franklin's decision to call for volunteers to defend Philadelphia from attack.

4. With respect to defense, *Spain having been several years at war against Britain, and being at length joined by France, which brought us into greater danger,* **and** *the labored and long-continued endeavors of our Governor Thomas to prevail with our Quaker Assembly to pass a militia law, and make other provisions for the security of the province having proved abortive,* I determined to try what might be done by a voluntary association of the people.

   a.

   b.

In short, an understanding of absolute constructions can help a reader navigate the deeper waters of high quality prose.

QUESTIONS

1. What did Franklin begin to publish in 1732? (PENGUIN 96)

   a. Title: _____

   b. Content: _____

2. What were Franklin's thoughts on the education of women? (PENGUIN 98)

3. Franklin was, at first, impressed with "a young Presbyterian minister named Hemphill," who immigrated from Ireland.

   a. What did Franklin particularly like about Hemphill? (PENGUIN 98)

   b. What did Hemphill do that caused Franklin to lose respect for him? (PENGUIN 99)

4. Franklin had little formal education and had not mastered Latin, which was routinely taught in schools in his time. What eventually "smoothed [his] way" in learning that language? (PENGUIN 99-100)

5. What was Franklin's advice to educators regarding foreign language instruction? (PENGUIN 100)

6. How did Franklin propose to expand the influence of the Junto? (PENGUIN 101-102)

7. What public offices did Franklin hold in 1736 and 1737? (PENGUIN 102-103)

8. Franklin turned his attention to public affairs. What components of city life was Franklin instrumental in establishing in Philadelphia?

   a. (PENGUIN 103-104) _____

   b. (PENGUIN 104) _____

   c. (PENGUIN 110) _____

   d. (PENGUIN 110) _____

9. What famous preacher from England made a strong impression on Franklin? What characteristic did Franklin particularly note in this man? (PENGUIN 108-109)

The Great Ideas: Opinion

One of the 102 Great Ideas laid out by Mortimer Adler is **Opinion.** In this reading, Franklin explains that people sometimes wanted him to publish something he regarded as "Libeling and Personal Abuse." They insisted that his newspaper *must* print their pieces because a newspaper was "like a Stage Coach in which any one who would pay had a Right to a Place" (PENGUIN 97). This gets to the heart of the "Liberty of the Press," which was later enshrined in the First Amendment to the Constitution of the United States. First, recount Franklin's belief on the obligation to print opinions with which he disagreed (PENGUIN 97). Second, indicate what you would consider to be the best way to guarantee the free expression of idea and opinions.

The Great Ideas: Virtue

One of the 102 Great Ideas laid out by Mortimer Adler is **Virtue.** In this part of the autobiography, Franklin continues to stress the importance of virtue and talks about his desire to establish a Society of the Free and Easy. Answer the series of graduated factual questions about his this organization, carrying the facts forward to the opinion question at the end.

Fact 1: Who would be eligible to join? (PENGUIN 94-95)

Fact 2: Before acceptance, what would newcomers be asked to do? (PENGUIN 95)

Fact 3: Why should the organization be kept secret? (PENGUIN 95)

Fact 4: What would members do for each other? (PENGUIN 95)

Fact 5: In what sense would members be "free"? (PENGUIN 95)

Opinion: Franklin states that such an organization "cannot fail." Do you agree? Why or why not?

Part 6: More Improvements

Scope

This reading covers pp. 112b-129a in the Penguin edition.

Terms

1. justice of the peace – an officer in colonial America who had judicial, executive, and legislative powers in matters exercised within a community; legal training not required

2. magistracy [MĂJ-ĭ-strə-sē] (n.) – the district of a magistrate, a minor official

3. sitting on the bench – doing the work of a judge (trying cases, interpreting law, passing sentence, etc.)

Words

4. extirpate [EX-tər-pāt] (v.) – to uproot; to destroy completely

5. rum [rəm] (n.) – alcoholic drink distilled from molasses and another sweetener such as sugar cane [Note: Europeans introduced alcoholic drinks such as beer and rum to Native Americans, who, according to recent research, metabolize enzyme variants differently, which may cause them to be more substance dependent.[8]]

Identifications

6. Dunkers (n.) – German Baptists who settled in Pennsylvania in 1723; called *tunkers* or *dunkers* for the German word for *immersion*

7. Spence (n.) – a Scottish lecturer whose first name appears to be unknown

8. Thomas (n.) – Governor George Thomas, who served as governor of Pennsylvania from 1738-47

Questions

1. What continued improvements and inventions are described in this section of the autobiography?

   a. _____ experiments (PENGUIN 120)

   b. establishment of a _____(PENGUIN 122)

   c. _____and _____the streets   (PENGUIN 125-26)

Illustration

Directions: Choose one of the bulleted subjects below. Then, in the space provided, make a sketch of what Franklin describes.

- The lamp Franklin invented to improve on the globe lamps from London (PENGUIN 126)

- Franklin's improvements to the London street design (PENGUIN 127-28)

The Great Ideas: Principle

1. One of the 102 Great Ideas laid out by Mortimer Adler is **Principle**. In this section, Benjamin Franklin talks about the conflict of conscience some Philadelphia Quakers felt when trying to maintain their principle of pacifism at a time period when the threat of Indian attack was very real. Answer the series of graduated factual questions about this situation, carrying the facts forward to the opinion question at the end.

Fact 1: As the city undertook to defend the city against Indian attack, what problem of conscience faced the Quakers? (PENGUIN 113)

Fact 2: How does Franklin describe the position of the Philadelphia Quakers on the issue of defense? Were they, for example, opposed to all war? (PENGUIN 113)

Fact 3: How did all involved use language to disguise Quaker compliance with the defense tax? (PENGUIN 115-16)

Opinion: Do you consider the Pennsylvania Quakers, who were living in a dangerous frontier area, to be hypocritical or practical by the use of language? Explain your answer.

The Great Ideas: Education

One of the 102 Great Ideas laid out by Mortimer Adler is **Education**. In this section, we read about the efforts of Benjamin Franklin and other Philadelphians to establish an academy in their city. Answer the series of graduated factual questions about their achievement, carrying the facts forward to the opinion question at the end.

Fact 1: How did the founders pay for the establishment of an academy (school)? (PENGUIN 118)

Fact 2: What facility did they use for the school? (PENGUIN 118-19)

Fact 3: How did they balance the influence of the city's various religious groups (sects) in administration of the school? (PENGUIN 119)

Fact 4: Was that arrangement 100% effective? (PENGUIN 119)

Fact 5: Did the governors of the school allow preachers to continue to use the site? (PENGUIN 119)

Fact 6: Did they allow children of the poor to attend the school? (PENGUIN 119)

Opinion: In this narrative, how would you characterize the relationship between church and state? How might this be instructive for our own time on the continuing issue of church-and-state in regard to schools? Explain your answer.

Connection

Answer the series of graduated factual questions about the events at Carlisle, carrying the facts forward to the connection at the end.

Fact 1: When the Philadelphians went to Carlisle to discuss a treaty with the Indians, what problem threatened to undermine the effort? (PENGUIN 121)

Fact 2: What did Franklin and the house speaker, Isaac Norris, do to prevent a disturbance? (PENGUIN 121)

Fact 3: After a rum-fueled public brawl broke out, what did the Indian counselor say with respect to Indian consumption of alcohol? (PENGUIN 122)

Fact 4: What rather startling comment did Franklin make about the eventual outcome of such a position? (PENGUIN 122)

Connection: To connect Franklin's comment to others of its kind through history, read the texts below and complete the response that follows.

Text 1

In the ancient Greek epic the Odyssey, *Odysseus' ship is blown off course to the land of the Lotus-eaters, who gave his men lotus flowers to eat. The result?*

"As soon as they tasted that honey-sweet fruit, they thought no more of coming back to us with news, but chose rather to stay there with the lotus-eating natives, and chew their lotus, and good-bye to home."[9]

Text 2

In China in 1836, during the Opium War, a member of the imperial council named Chu Tsun was observing the behavior of the British toward both India and China and advised the Daoguang (Tao-kuang) Emperor, thus:

Chinese Opium Den, 1896

"The people called Hungmaou (Red Haired) came hither, and, having manufactured opium, seduced some of the nations into the habit of smoking it: from these the mania for it spread through the whole nation, so that in process of time the nation became feeble and enervated, submitted to the foreign rule, and ultimately were completely subjugated. Now the English are of the race of foreigners called Hungmaou. In introducing opium into the country their purpose has been to weaken and enfeeble the central empire. If not early aroused to a sense of our danger, we shall find ourselves, ere long, on the last step towards ruin."[10]

Text 3

In Great Britain in 1985, at the time the drug culture was expanding across Europe, Prime Minister Margaret Thatcher (1925-2013) said:

Prime Minister Margaret Thatcher

"Britain—like the rest of Europe—is up against a determined effort to flood the country with hard drugs to corrupt our youth—to undermine the stability of the country."[11]

Response: With your classmates (or in a paragraph), determine the common theme of all these passages, including Ben Franklin's comments about rum and the Native American population. Do you think the speakers/writers are on to something, or are the remarks simply examples of either entertainment or xenophobia? What are the implications for our own country in our own time? Is there any solution to this long-lived suspicion and fear?

Part 7: The French and Indian War

Scope

This reading covers pp. 130-154a in the Penguin edition.

Terms

1. bond (n.) – a promise to pay a debt within a certain time

2. loophole (n.) – a narrow opening in the wall of a fortification for the purpose of firing upon the enemy

3. palisade [păl-ə-SĀD] (n., usually pl.) – a fence of wooden stakes creating an enclosure for the purpose of protection from enemies or predators

Words

4. ambuscade [ăm-bəs-KĀD or ĂM-bəs-kād] (n.) (*now obsolete*) attack from an ambush

5. per diem [pər DĒ-əm] (adv. phr.) – Latin for "per day"

6. prerogative [prē-RŎG-ə-tĭv] (n.) – a right or privilege that belongs to a certain class of people

Identifications

7. Bethlehem (n.) – Bethlehem, Pennsylvania; site of a Moravian mission to Native Americans, founded in 1741

8. Braddock (n.) – Edward Braddock (1695-1755), British military General defeated in the French and Indian War

9. Dunbar (n.) – Colonel Thomas Dunbar (d. 1767), Braddock's second in command

10. Gnadenhut [zhĭ-NĀ-dən-hət or NĂ-dən-hət] (n.) – (*now Gnadenhutten*) site of a Moravian mission to Native Americans, founded in 1746; German for "cabins of grace"

11. Northwest frontier (n.) – the border between French and English possessions during the French and Indian War (see map)

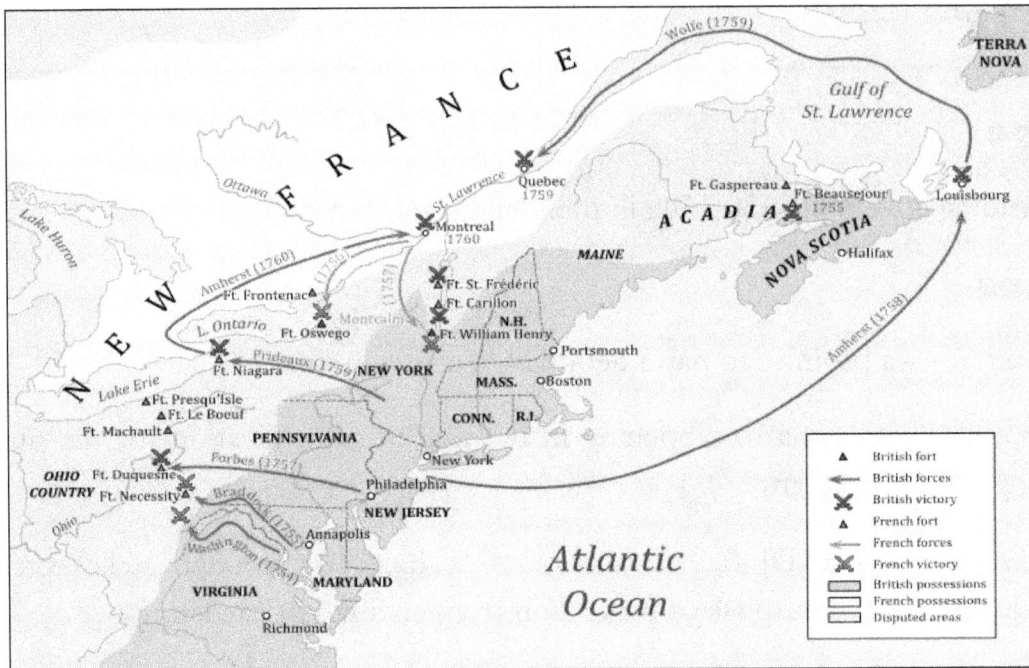

European territories during the French and Indian War (1754-1763), showing the French in the lighter color (NW) and the English in the darker (coastal), and disputed territory between the two

12. Sancho Panza [SÄN-chō PÄN-zə] – a fictional character in the novel *Don Quixote* by Miguel de Cervantes, published in 1605

13. the Six Nations – the Six Nations Confederacy, a coalition of Native American tribes including the Seneca, Cayuga, Onondaga, Oneida, Mohawk, and Tuscarora

14. Monongahela [mə-NÖNG-gə-HÄ-lə] – the Monongahela River, which flows 128 miles from NW Virginia through SW Pennsylvania into the Ohio River

Questions

1. In 1754, as the war with France began to spill onto the American continent, with whom did the Congress of Commissioners meet in Albany? Why? (PENGUIN 130)

2. At that time, twenty-six years before the Revolutionary War, Franklin proposed a union of all the colonies under one government. In the next four questions, explain what he said about his plan? (PENGUIN 130-31)

    a. Who would administer the general government, and how would he be chosen? (PENGUIN 131)

    b. Along with this individual, who else would administer the government? How would they be chosen? (PENGUIN 131)

    c. Why were the assemblies opposed to the plan? (PENGUIN 131)

    d. Why were the English opposed to the plan? (PENGUIN 131)

3. What two decisions by Col. Thomas Dunbar caused the Americans to suspect that the British Regulars were not as tough as they had previously thought? (PENGUIN 143)

    a. _____

    b. _____

4. Another dispute arose regarding taxation to pay for the war effort. Briefly summarize the contrasting positions of the Proprietaries and the Assemblies? Who won out in the end? (PENGUIN 145-46)

5. What defenses did the inhabitants of Bethlehem, Pennsylvania, devise as protection against the Indians, who had attacked Gnadenhut? (PENGUIN 147)

    a. The main buildings were protected by _____.

    b. _____and _____ had been purchased.

    c. They had placed a number of _____between the windows of their high stone houses so that _____

6. Briefly summarize what happened to the eleven farmers to whom Franklin gave firearms. (PENGUIN 147-48)

7. Use the diagram of graduated questions below to size up Franklin's talents.

Fact 1: When General Braddock needed wagons, Franklin proposed to get them in Pennsylvania. In a few words, indicate what Franklin proposed in his advertisement. (PENGUIN 136-37)

Fact 2: When the inhabitations of the counties of Lancaster, York, and Cumberland balked at letting go of their wagons, what sensible solution did Franklin conceive? (PENGUIN 138-39)

Fact 3: When the owners of the wagons and horses said they feared Braddock would not pay, what did Franklin do? (PENGUIN 139)

Fact 4: When the Committee of Assembly was preparing to furnish soldiers with food, what did Franklin recommend (on his son's advice)? (PENGUIN 140)

Fact 5: When the chaplain said the soldiers were not attending his sermons regularly, what solution did Franklin propose? (PENGUIN 150)

Opinion: Considering Franklin's various solutions to the problems facing the colonists, what word or phrase would you use to describe him?

The Great Ideas: War

Opposing Troops in Traditional European Formation

One of the 102 Great Ideas laid out by Mortimer Adler is **War**. Franklin describes the defeat of the British General Edward Braddock (1695-1755), who was sent to the colonies to engage the French and their Indian allies. Franklin explains how Braddock, "a brave Man" who "might probably have made a Figure as a good Officer in some European War," failed utterly in his conflict with the Indians in the battle on the Monongahela. On another piece of paper, explain in your own words why this happened. For example, what personality traits were disadvantageous? How was fighting in America different from fighting in Europe (see illustration above)?

Research

The Gnadenhutten Massacre

NOTE: *This research can be undertaken if your teacher assigns it or if you simply wish to learn more about conflicts between Native Americans and colonists. The descriptions of the violence are heart-rending and should be approached prayerfully.*

In the context of the French and Indian War, Franklin recounts an Indian assault at "Gnadenhut" (Gnadenhutten) and the aftermath (PENGUIN 146-47). That incident happened in 1755. Probably more frequently mentioned in history books is the Gnadenhutten Massacre of March 8, 1782. At that time, a group of armed Pennsylvanians descended upon the Gnadenhutten mission and massacred 96 Christian Indians from the Lenape tribe. Motivated by revenge for outrages committed on their families, the attackers were indiscriminate and felt certain the peaceful Lenape were protecting the Indians who had been on the attack. The Christian mission at Gnadenhutten was founded by a Moravian Christian named David Zeisberger (1721-1808), a passionate advocate for the rights of Native Americans. Because of his advocacy for the Lenape and others, he was arrested by the British and held at Fort Detroit. The massacre happened during the period of his imprisonment.

Interesting sources which bear on this matter are available on the Internet and in many libraries. We will focus on the following:

1. **De Schweinitz, Edmund. *The Life and Times of David Zeisberger, the Western Pioneer and Apostle to the Indians.* Philadelphia: Lippincott, 1870.**

   a. The incident of 1755 is narrated on pp. 230-40.

   b. The incident of 1782 is narrated on pp. 537-52.

   Available on the web site *Internet Archive*. The URL is: <https://archive.org/stream/cihm_26078#page/n5/mode/2up>.

   (NOTE: The microform format is recommended over the full text option, which is often full of typos due to the digital formatting.)

2. **Letter from Benjamin Franklin to James Hutton, 7 July 1782.**

   Available on the web site *National Archives*. The URL is <http://founders.archives.gov/documents/Franklin/01-37-02-0377>.

Begin by reading the two suggested excerpts from Schweinitz's book. Then read Benjamin Franklin's letter to James Hutton, in which he makes strong comments about the massacre. When finished, write a four-paragraph essay according to this format:

Paragraph 1: Summarize the 1755 incident

Paragraph 2: Summarize the 1782 incident

Paragraph 3: Compare Franklin's responses to the two incidents.

Paragraph 4: Express your own thoughts about the two incidents. Could they have been avoided? How? Are racial tensions better, worse, or about the same in our own time? What is the proper Christian position on the balance between defense and aggression?

Part 8: Leadership

Scope

This reading covers pp. 154b-171 in the Penguin edition.

Terms

1. packet (n.) – (*now obsolete*) a ship that carries mail at regular intervals between two ports

2. solicitor [sə-LĬS-ĭ-tər] (n.) – an English or Welsh legal representative (attorney) who advises clients, represents them in the lower courts, and prepares cases for a barrister, a different kind of attorney who then takes them before the higher courts

Words

3. equity [Ĕ-kwĭt-ē] (n.) – the quality of being fair and impartial

4. odium [Ō-dē-əm] (n.) – hatred or intense dislike

Identifications

5. F.R.S. – Fellow (member) of the Royal Society

6. Loudon [LĂŪ-dən] – John Campbell, 4th Earl of Loudon (1705-1782), a British army officer

7. Madeira [mə-DĬ-rə] – a Portuguese wine made on the island of Madeira, off the coast of Morocco

8. Royal Academy of Sciences – a learned society of scientists, established in France by King Louis XIV in 1666 for the promotion of scientific research

9. Royal Society – a learned society of scientists, established in Great Britain by King Charles II in 1660 for the promotion of scientific research; full name: The President, Council, and Fellows of the Royal Society of London for Improving Natural Knowledge

10. Scilly Isles [SĬL-ē īlz] – a group of small islands (or archipelago) off the southwestern tip of Cornwall (England)

11. Shirley – Governor William Shirley (1694-1771), a British colonial governor

12. St. George's Channel – the channel of water between Ireland and Wales (see circled area on map)

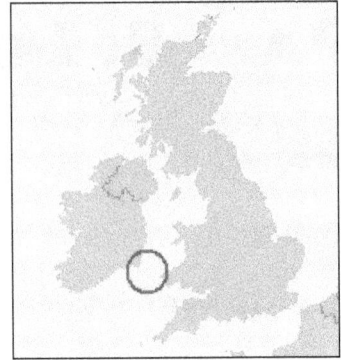

St. George's Channel

Questions

1. The English scientist Peter Collinson presented a gift to Franklin for use in his electric experiments. What was it? (PENGUIN 154)

2. How did Collinson help Franklin's scientific research to be introduced to Europe? (PENGUIN 155)

3. What honor, rare for an American, was extended to Franklin as a result of his experiments in electricity? (PENGUIN 157)

4. The conflict between the Proprietaries and the Assembly members continues. The Governor William Denny pressured Franklin to give up the opposition to the tax-free status of the Proprietaries. What was Franklin's response? (PENGUIN 158)

5. Franklin reflects on a problem with shipping in his day. The same ship, handled by different captains and crews, would perform differently—some quicker, some slower. What did Franklin propose to overcome this problem? (PENGUIN 165-66)

6. When near the English coast, the ship in which Franklin was traveling narrowly escaped shipwreck. What invention saved them and led Franklin to say they should be building more in America? (PENGUIN 167)

7. Use the diagram of graduated questions on the next page to examine Franklin's thoughts on leadership.

Fact 1: What weaknesses did Franklin believe made Lord Loudon a poor leader? (PENGUIN 160-62)

Fact 2: By contrast, what qualities did Franklin admire in General William Shirley? (PENGUIN 163)

Fact 3: When Franklin requested that Lord Loudon reimburse him for money he had lent for public affairs, how did Loudon respond? (PENGUIN 164)

Fact 4: Franklin explains that Parliament had promised to advocate for the colonists in the colonists' interpretation of the King's "laws." Did Parliament come through? Explain your answer. (PENGUIN 168)

Fact 5: The Proprietaries employed as their solicitor (attorney) Ferdinando John Paris. What shortcomings did Franklin see in Paris's style? (PENGUIN 169)

Fact 6: When Governor Denny proposed an act requiring the Proprietaries to be taxed, the council meeting seemed to be in a deadlock. How did William Murray, Earl of Mansfield, create a resolution? (PENGUIN 170-71)

Perception: In conclusion, how would you describe Franklin's ideal leader? Do you agree with him? Why or why not?

Bible Connection

One of the reasons Benjamin Franklin was so invaluable in the founding of Philadelphia and the United States was his skill in leadership. Look up the passages of Scripture listed below and, in the space provided, indicate the element of good leadership which the Bible provides us.

1. Philippians 2:3 _____

2. Matthew 20:28 _____

3. Proverbs 19:20 _____ and _____

4. Proverbs 3:5 _____

5. Proverbs 13:4 _____

Progymnasmata: Chreia

Benjamin Franklin is well known for his wise sayings, many of which were gathered together in his publication *Poor Richard's Almanack*. Three sayings that bear directly on this section of the autobiography are these:

- Never leave that till tomorrow which you can do today.

- He that can have patience can have what he will.

- Make yourselves sheep and the wolves will eat you.

Discuss the sayings together as a class, looking for examples from this section of the autobiography. Choose one of the three sayings above, and write a chreia (an explication of the wise saying). To write a chreia, follow the eight steps on the next page, writing one paragraph for each.

Steps in a Chreia

Paragraph	Content
1. Citation	State the quote inside quotation marks and tell the name of the person who said it.
2. Encomium	Praise the wisdom of the person who originated the saying.
3. Paraphrase	Restate the proverb in your own words.
4. Cause-Effect	Explain why the saying is wise. What are its benefits?
5. Contrast	Indicate a position opposite the one you are explaining.
6. Comparison	Explain the concept by comparing it to something that is more familiar to the reader.
7. Example	Give an example from fact or fiction to prove the truth of the saying.
8. Testimony of the Ancients	Quote an authority from the past who expressed the same idea.

A model chreia appears on the next page to show how these steps might appear in the final composition.

How to Make Enemies

Citation + Encomium + Paraphrase

Benjamin Franklin was very wise when he said, "He makes a foe, who makes a jest." This means that when we make fun of someone, we turn him or her into an enemy.

Contrast

Another quotation by Benjamin Franklin shows a better way to interact with others: "Do good to thy friend to keep him, to thy enemy to gain him."

Comparison

Franklin's statement is true in the animal world, too. If a cat hisses threateningly at a puppy, the puppy will avoid the cat from then on. The cat has made a foe.

Cause-Effect

Franklin's observation is wise because it explains how a thoughtless remark can have years of consequences that may extend far beyond the two people involved in the initial "jest."

Example

One example of Franklin's observation was played out on the world stage. In the early twentieth century, a little boy in Germany started school. Unfortunately, he walked with a limp and wore a metal brace on his right leg because of a birth defect. The other children would make fun of him, and he grew up with a horrible anger inside him. The boy was Joseph Goebbels, who became the propaganda minister for Adolph Hitler in the 1930s. Some believe that the unkindness he met as a child was avenged in the Holocaust. We may well be seeing the truth of Franklin's aphorism in Goebbels' life.

Testimony of the Ancients

Franklin's aphorism is supported by the Bible. In his epistle, James points out that the tongue "is a restless evil, full of deadly poison" (3:8); and Proverbs shows the influence of our words on others: "A soft answer turns away wrath, but a harsh word stirs up anger" (15:1). This supports Franklin's idea that we need to use our words kindly to create a civil society.

Notes

[1] "The Fifth Theological Oration on the Holy Spirit." Christian Classics Ethereal Library. 13 July 2005. Web. 22 Jan. 2016.

[2] "Philosophy Is Everybody's Business." *TheGreatIdeas.org*. The Great Ideas. Center for the Study of the Great Ideas: A Synoptical Approach to the Great Books and Practical Philosophy. Web. 12 Jan. 2016.

[3] Roget. 3rd ed. New York: Crowell, 1962. 437, 84.

[4] Gabriel-Honoré de Riquetti, "The Elegy on Franklin." *A Library of the World's Best Literature: Ancient and Modern."* Ed. Charles Dudley Warner. New York: International Society, 1896. 25.10086.

[5] *Benjamin Franklin.* New York: Viking, 1938. 779.

[6] *Letters Concerning the English Nation.* London: Davis, Lyon, 1733. 29.

[7] Addison, Joseph. *The Works of Joseph Addison.* New York: Harper, 1837. 1.31.

[8] C. L. Ehlers and I. R. Gizer. Abstract of "Evidence for a Genetic Component for Substance Dependence in Native Americans." *American Journal of Psychiatry*. Feb. 2013. National Center for Biotechnology Information. n.d. Web. 2 Nov. 2015.

[9] Homer. "How Odysseus Visited the Lotus Eaters and the Cyclops." *Odyssey.* Ed. W. H. D. Rouse. 1937. New York: Mentor-New American, 1963. 9.102.

[10] "The Opium Question and the Suspended Trade with China." *Fraser's Magazine for Town and Country*. March 1840. 2:370. 5 Sept. 2014. Web. 21 Oct. 2015.

[11] Pryce, Sue. *Fixing Drugs: The Politics of Drug Prohibition.* London: Palgrave Macmillan, 2012. 13. n.d. Web. 22 Oct. 2015.

Attribution for Licensed Images

www.ingramcontent.com/pod-product-compliance
Lightning Source LLC
Chambersburg PA
CBHW081152040426
42445CB00015B/1850